Jonathan Holt saw his first folly in Dorset at the age of sixteen, remaining in the county long enough to appreciate the fact that its landscape does not need improving by the construction of follies. He lectures on the subject in adult education, organises tours and conferences, and writes for several publications, including *Follies*, the organ of the Folly Fellowship, a charity dedicated to architectural conservation, of which he was South West Region Secretary from 1990 to 1996. In 1997 he moved to Bath, the most densely follied city in Britain.

Following page
Dorset's greatest folly builder was undoubtedly
George Burt, who during the second half of the nineteenth
century transformed Swanage, filling his home town with
buildings from London. This is the Wellington Clock Tower near
Peveril Point, which originally stood at the
southern approach to London Bridge.

DISCOVER DORSET

FOLLIES

JONATHAN HOLT

THE DOVECOTE PRESS

To Nathalie, without whose support, understanding and patience, this book might never have seen the light of day

The bas-relief of a face fringed with icicles over
the House of Winter pavilion, Athelhampton.

First published in 2000 by The Dovecote Press Ltd
Stanbridge, Wimborne, Dorset BH21 4JD

ISBN 1 874336 71 7

© Jonathan Holt 2000

Jonathan Holt has asserted his rights under the Copyright, Designs
and Patent Act 1988 to be identified as author of this work

Series designed by Humphrey Stone

Typeset in Monotype Sabon
Printed and bound by Baskerville Press, Salisbury, Wiltshire

A CIP catalogue record for this book is available
from the British Library

1 3 5 7 9 8 6 4 2

CONTENTS

INTRODUCTION 7

THE FOLLIES 10

Athelhampton – Bournemouth – Brownsea Island

Charborough Park – Compton Acres – Creech

Duntish Court – Encombe – Horton – Kimmeridge

Kingston Lacy – Kingston Maurward

Lillington – Lulworth – Mapperton

Melbury Sampford – Milton Abbas

Milborne St Andrew - Moreton – Portesham

Sherborne - Stalbridge – Swanage

Wimborne Minster – Wimborne St Giles

FURTHER READING 78

ACKNOWLEDGEMENTS 79

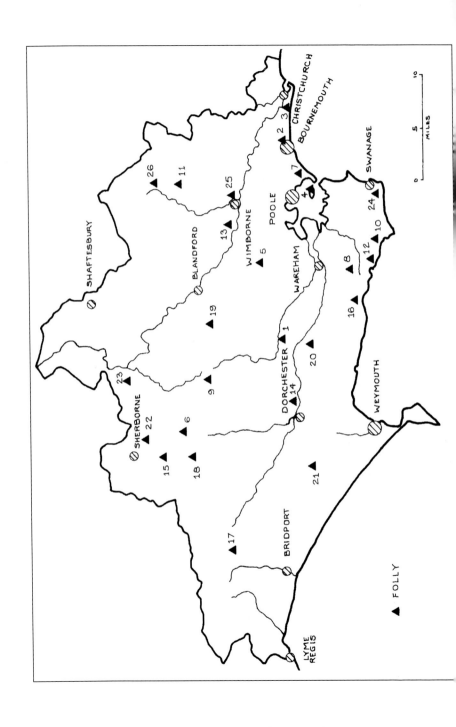

SHAFTESBURY

CHRISTCHURCH

BOURNEMOUTH

2
3
7

26

11

POOLE

25

SWANAGE

4

BLANDFORD

WIMBORNE

13

24

10

5

12

WAREHAM

8

19

16

DORCHESTER

1

23

9

14

20

SHERBORNE

22

WEYMOUTH

15

6

18

21

17

BRIDPORT

FOLLY

LYME
REGIS

0   5   10

MILES

INTRODUCTION

Dorset offers many delights, including a dramatic coastline, thatched cottages in unspoilt villages and historic churches that stretch halfway to Heaven. A bicycle and inquiring mind are all one needs to explore 'a face on which time makes but little impression', as Thomas Hardy described one part of the county, Egdon Heath. It was with these two weapons in my armoury that I set forth, aged sixteen, and discovered my first follies.

My initiation was Horton Tower, whose red-brick mass towered over me. Inevitably, these bigger examples first attracted my attention, but soon the smaller and equally fascinating curiosities such as Denis Bond's Creech Arch and George Burt's Great Globe were 'collected' like prize gems in a stamp collection. Another memorable event was my guarding Charborough Tower against a horde of ravaging Rotarians for fear they would cause damage to the weakened fabric. It was liberating to explore the highways and byways of this sweeping landscape and the more I did so, the more I became drawn into an

Map of Dorset Follies: 1. Athelhampton (pavilions & dovecote); 2. Bournemouth: centre (watertower); 3. Bournemouth: Southbourne (shell garden); 4. Brownsea Island (arcade & towers; gazebo); 5. Charborough (tower & icehouse); 6. Holnest (site of mausoleum); 7. Canford Cliffs: Compton Acres (Imperial Tea House & summerhouse; 8. Creech (arch); 9. Duntish (grotto);10. Encombe (rock arch, obelisk & temple); 11. Horton (tower); 12. Kimmeridge (tower); 13. Kingston Lacy (obelisks); 14. Kingston Maurward (gazebo & temple); 15. Lillington (tower); 16. Lulworth (lodges & shamfort); 17. Mapperton (pool house); 18. Melbury Sampford (grotto, gardenhouse & tower); 19. Milton Abbas (sham chapel); 20. Moreton (obelisk); 21. Portesham (monument); 22. Sherborne (sham tower & wall); 23. Stalbridge (obelisk); 24. Swanage (globe, obelisks, columns, arch, pavilion, tower, statues, façade, gazebo); 25. Wimborne Minster (gazebo); 26. Wimborne St Giles (grotto, tower & gateway).

exploration of its architectural highlights. Serious research for this book, including days on end at the Dorset Record Office and other archives, came much later, after I had moved out of the county and I was able to observe its qualities more objectively.

In comparison to other counties, Dorset is not rich in follies, though the best are equal to any in England. Gwyn Headley and Wim Meulenkamp conclude in their masterwork, simply entitled *Follies*, that the eighteenth century 'passed Dorset by', by which they mean that few of its country estates were reshaped in the English landscape style, a movement which gave birth to much architectural eccentricity. This is not entirely true, for some were redesigned, others created from scratch, notably Sherborne Castle and St Giles House near Wimborne. Perhaps closer to the truth is the fact that Dorset never was a county of great houses whose owners poured vast sums into the follification of their estates. The few families that did own large estates, such as the Bankes or Welds, rarely interested themselves in landscaping and only flirtingly indulged in folly building.

The building of follies in a rural landscape is only telling part of the story, for many can be found in suburban gardens, by the sea, or on high streets in the middle of towns. Furthermore, by their very nature, real follies are illogical and apparently useless, and so planning their construction could be considered a contradiction. Nevertheless, I have included in this book examples of unusual garden buildings, such as gazebos and summer-houses, which may equally be part of a grand design or simply the less extravagant expression of someone's individuality or artistic flair.

A world of styles can be found in the county's parks and gardens - Japanese, Roman, Gothic, Italianate, Greek, as well as a variety of building types - shell houses, columns, obelisks, arches, gatehouses and sham ruins. And there are some fine towers, often prominent, sometimes an expression of *folie de grandeur*, as at Charborough Park, or commemorative in some way, like the Hardy Monument above Portesham. Intimacy and femininity are also expressed, notably in the grottoes at St Giles' House, Duntish Court and Melbury Sampford. There is no 'story of follies' with a beginning, a middle and an end. Generally they sprang up, and still do appear, in a quirky, haphazard way.

If there is one builder who stands out among all those who have left their mark in the form of a folly, it is George Burt (1816-1894). Driven by a desire to educate and edify his fellow citizens of Swanage, he did not wish to restrict the enjoyment of his embellishments to a closed circle of friends - like some landowners. Burt's bits of fancy were for all to enjoy, and hopefully, learn about the world. There are stone plaques packed with chronological, geophysical and astronomical data, or quotes from Shakespeare and other poets. Burt was a direct descendant of those high-minded aesthetes who wished to create arcadias on Earth, ideal lands flowing with milk and honey and peopled by gods and nymphs reclining around nymphaea, gazing from gazebos and making libations in temples. Perhaps this book should be dedicated to George Burt, the ordinary man who made good, and built a fantasyland without the benefit of much education or travelling in Italy and Greece, the classical world from which many follies derive.

Some of Dorset's follies are in good condition and well looked after, cared for by both private individuals and major national organizations like the National Trust. Others are neglected and largely forgotten, and I can only hope that this book will in some small way halt the decline in their fortunes. For example, the grotto at St Giles' House is an important early example of shell and coral work, and although its basic structure will probably be standing in ten years time because it is in a relatively sheltered site, its once magnificent interior will gradually decay. Other follies face a more visible fate, notably the Clavel Tower at Kimmeridge. Not only are strong winds likely to dislodge the stones with which it is built, but cliff erosion is on the point of eating away its foundations - and the tower will simply fall into the sea. Fortunately, the Folly Fellowship, a charity dedicated to the saving and preservation of follies, grottoes and garden buildings, is in a position to alert the appropriate authorities and help formulate a management plan, thus preserving these small but always delightful examples of our architectural heritage.

Follies are often a joyful expression of a desire to be different, to be noticed, to make a statement. Even if we lack the desire, space, or money to build one ourselves, there is nothing to stop us learning about follies and tracking them down for ourselves, a purpose this book hopefully fulfils.

THE FOLLIES

ATHELHAMPTON
(OS REF: 194 SY 771 942)

Athelhampton is one of Dorset's most ancient manor houses, a favoured spot next to the River Piddle where Sir William Martyn settled and completed the Great Hall in 1485, the year of the Battle of Bosworth and accession of Henry VII. Martyn was a Lord Mayor of London and Master of the Skinners' Company, and his family carried on adding wings and outbuildings after his death.

Several other families have since owned the estate, but since 1957 it has been in the care of the Cooke family and remains one of the most impressive manor houses in the county. The grounds consist of a number of charming enclosed gardens, each on a different theme or with a distinct look. There are pools and fountains, statues abound of various gods including Apollo and Hygea, and Queen Victoria in all her majesty.

The look of a large part of the gardens today is due to Alfred Cart de Lafontaine, a Frenchman who between 1891 and 1899 carefully restored the house and employed one of the most inspired garden designers of the day, Francis Inigo Thomas. Thomas's main feature is the Great Court, where a series of pyramidal yew hedges taper sharply to a point. The house can be glimpsed in the middle distance, whilst along the southern edge of the court he built the South Terrace and the pavilions, facing each other and overlooking the garden beneath.

The approach to both pavilions is up a flight of steps half way along a terrace whose balustrade is punctuated at intervals by short obelisks. A dark ochre variety of Ham Stone from Somerset is used in the pavilions, which are essentially identical, except that the one at the western end of the terrace, called the House of Joy or the House of

The House of Summer; one of the pavilions at Athelhampton.

The sixteenth century dovecote, Athelhampton.

Summer, has a smiling face over its door, while the eastern house has a tortured face surrounded by icicles and is called the House of Sorrow or the House of Winter. The buildings have Corinthian capitals on each corner and a ball pinnacle on a pyramidal roof, echoing the neighbouring yew hedges. Sculpted into a cartouche on the entablature are the letters 'ACL' after their creator. Originally the pavilions were just lovely places to while away a hot afternoon. They also served a practical purpose - to house the water tanks supplying water to the fountains, but the tanks have been removed and the water flow is controlled electrically.

Apart from the pavilions, the other outbuilding of interest is the dovecote, a large circular structure dating from the early sixteenth century, which would have provided meat for the family and fertiliser in the form of dung for the garden. Built mainly of coarse rubble, it has buttresses supporting the wall at regular intervals around the outside, and is about 22 feet in diameter and 25 feet high. The doorway is very low - about two feet six inches high. The door is now normally ajar, inviting you in to admire the magnificent range of some 600 pigeonholes. It was restored by Blandford architect Aylmer Howard in 1971, but only after a piece of silverware had been sold at Christie's to meet the cost. At the crown of the conical roof a new lantern was built by E.W. Kingsbury & Sons of Poole, complete with ledges for birds. Soon afterwards the copper ball finial was bent over in a gale, which is how it has remained ever since. The potence, or wooden pole, which would have originally had lateral arms and a ladder for collecting eggs, lies sadly on the ground inside.

BOURNEMOUTH

Bournemouth was built too late to take advantage of the folly-building boom. In the eighteenth century it was little more than a fishing village next to a narrow river mouth. Nevertheless, and despite the town's rapid growth, a couple of very different follies have survived intact, the oldest of which forms part of what might be considered a typically 'Bournemouthian' landscape. This is the Water Tower (OS REF: 195 SZ 078 917) in the Upper Gardens by the Bourne stream, which stands in

The Victorian Water Tower in the Upper Gardens, Bournemouth.

grounds developed by the Durrant family, and forms part of a narrow two-mile-long series of gardens inspired by John Claudius Loudon's conception of the 'gardenesque'. There is a mixture of lawns, winding paths, formal bedding, and a variety of trees, which being Bournemouth, are predominantly pines. Peeping through those trees are villas in private grounds, but the only building of note within the gardens is the Water Tower.

The first time that the tower appeared in an illustration was in 1890 in an engraving by a W.J. Warren entitled 'In Miss Durrant's Garden, looking North-West'. It is likely that George Durrant was responsible for the tower, for Mate's *Bournemouth Illustrated* in 1893 suggests that despite leasing the land to the municipality, he drained the grounds and continued to landscape them, laying out features such as a water wheel, now gone. Excavations have not substantiated the theory that the wheel was used for lifting water into the tower, which until the arrival of mains water in 1940 acted as a reservoir for irrigating the lawns and flowers and feeding a nearby pond and fountain.

The thirty feet high tower is bristling with features more typical of the Middle Ages than late-Victorian Bournemouth, including crenellations, machicolations and arrow slits. All in red brick, it stands next to a fine lawn which slopes down to the Bourne stream.

Bournemouth's other folly is altogether different, more of a *jardin imaginaire* or an open-air exhibition of the mollusc art crammed into a small space. George Howard (1898-1985), who did not have the means of Durrant, was in turn a coal-miner, a member of the Irish Constabulary, and served in both World Wars. Settling eventually in Bournemouth in about 1948 in a pebble-dash house at 137 Overcliff Drive, Southbourne (OS REF: 195 SZ 142 913), which has a view directly onto the sea, he created something that any ordinary man could do with a little imagination. We do not know what motivated him, but the Shell Garden remains a glorious example of extended fancy or conceit, and despite its modest setting is not so far removed in spirit from the creations of aristocrats with deeper pockets and more space to play with.

The initial impression to the casual passer-by is one of chaos, with every square inch filled with shells - which Howard once described as

A general view of 137 Overcliff Drive, Southbourne.

'the only things in this world that grow more beautiful after death'. National and other themes are placed cheek by jowl, and there are various cornucopias of shells, rocks, stones and ceramics. The only substantial building is the Chapel, approached down some steps inset with religious icons, such as Christ with his crown of thorns and the Virgin Mary, as well as views of churches, often on plates bought at the gift shop of some shrine or other. Outside, gaiety flourishes with a series of ponds, model ships, statues, a windmill and most intriguing of all, a Cave of Curios, a sort of display cabinet where rock specimens are labelled in letters made of broken glass and beads. 'East or West, Home Sweet Home is Best' is just one of many aphorisms which litter this site - along with stones and rocks from various parts of the world, including the St Gotthard Pass (Switzerland), Port Blair (Borneo) and the Gulf of Eilat (Israel). Like many others before and since, Howard also plundered the Acropolis!

His excuse for such light-fingered behaviour may have been that he did it for charity, hoping that visitors would put their loose change in a collecting box in support of worthy causes such as Cancer Research, or the Howard Centre at Christchurch Hospital, the unit named in recognition of his fund-raising. The seeds of the Shell Garden were first sown in 1948, when George Howard was still in the Merchant

Part of the Shell Garden, Southbourne.

Navy. Not conceiving how it would finally turn out, he collected what he could as he sailed the world, working single-handed on the project after settling in Southbourne. In the Philippines, he set his heart on a giant clam shell weighing four and a half hundredweight, and for which he had to wait seven years until it was transported to Bournemouth. Once the Shell Garden was established and his reputation began to spread, people sent shells to help him complete its various sections.

Although George Howard may have lacked the obsessive single-mindedness of Ferdinand Cheval, the French village postman who built his Palais Idéal out of anything he could pick off the ground on his rounds in the Département of Drôme, Howard took as long - some 32 years. He also used a comparable amount of material - including one million shells - creating a monument that benefited from new materials such as artificial pearls and glazed ceramics, materials rarely available to the eighteenth century shell and rock artists who first started the craze for grottoes and shell houses.

BROWNSEA ISLAND

(OS REF: 195 SZ 032 876)

Brownsea Island lies at a strategic point in Poole Harbour, in a perfect position to defend Poole against marauding invaders and with this aim in view a fort was built on the island in about 1545, towards the end of Henry VIII's reign. It was on Brownsea that in 1907 Lord Baden Powell pitched his first Boy Scout camp, and its pastoral charms and fresh sea breeze have won over numerous other visitors. As one Victorian clergyman wrote, in *A Sketch of Brownsea Island* (1881), '. . . it means no catching of trains, no school-boards, . . . or burglaries, no election fights, no insubordination, squalor or poverty.'

Thus the stage was set for a Prospero to conjure up a few follies, and by the time the National Trust took over the island in 1963 several owners had added to its natural magic. The first of these were Sir Gerard Napier and Humphrey Sturt who acquired the island in 1762. Sturt, or his father according to some accounts, had already left his mark on Dorset's landscape by building the Horton Tower, the seven-storey folly north of Wimborne. After the death of Napier, Sturt

Brownsea Castle and Island from Poole Harbour, with the two watch towers on the Family Pier prominent on the left.

made additions to the castle, created some large plantations of trees, built hothouses and an ornamental park, spending £50,000 on these transformations.

The next owner to leave his impact on Brownsea was Colonel William Petrie Waugh, who bought the island in 1852, principally for its clay, which he had been told had the right properties for making the finest porcelain. After considerable investment, including the building of a large pottery works, he was finally disillusioned, for the clay was found to be only good enough for sewage pipes and sanitary ware.

The mark he left on the island's architecture was more lasting, for he added a front in the Tudor Gothic style to the castle, as well as various towers and turrets, including the clock tower on the gatehouse and the turret in red brick which lours over the drive.

His fishing temple on the upper lake has now gone, but there remains his curious architectural ensemble by the waterside known as the Family Pier. The visitor approaching the main quay at the east end of the island first sees the two watch towers whose cream paint glistens in the sun. Beyond them lies what appears to be a sham wall with false windows connecting the towers to the land. This is in fact the Crystal Arcade, which derives its name from being lit from above by a glass roof, and which is approached from the Castle's Italian garden. The purpose of the ensemble seems to have been multiple: firstly to create a place from which to bathe for Colonel Waugh's family; secondly to provide a landing-stage; thirdly to provide storage for garden implements; and fourthly, most spuriously, to act as a look-out for marauding invaders and any other seafaring folk.

It was not until Augustus Cavendish Bentinck, MP for Whitehaven, bought the island in 1870 that the Crystal Arcade became truly embellished. He was an Italophile, and transported to Brownsea a number of artefacts of Italian origin. One might guess that his favourite city was Venice from the number of sixteenth and seventeenth century Venetian stone carvings he placed in the arcade, including three bearing the city's symbol of the winged Lion of St Mark, as well as fifteen shields of arms, sculptures of various deities such as Pan, Flora, Ceres, Hebe and Hercules, as well as a water nymph. Such was its air of sanctity that the children of Charles van Raalte, a later owner, called it 'The Vatican'.

The gazebo, Brownsea Castle.

These were virtually all removed on Bentinck's death, except for one winged lion, a Russian eagle, several griffins and a preaching angel. There are false cross-slits too, whilst the arcade's sense of theatre is heightened by the windows at the end, with their sea views. Beyond the window lies the landing stage, which is reached through a door to the left. Set into its concrete is a large compass, whilst above the door there is a stone panel sculpted with another winged lion. Yet another winged lion is featured on a larger stone immediately above, and forms part of the crenellation of the parapet which runs between the two twenty-feet towers. These are identical, and have false windows, as well as real drip mouldings and crenellations, thus acting as a foretaste of the castle in their rear.

As for other interesting garden buildings, in the ornamental gardens on the west side of the castle, which Cavendish Bentinck named Venetia Park after his daughter, there was once a long conservatory stretching out across what is now lawn. It was also evident, according to a guide book, that 'ornamental works [were] of frequent occurrence' and there was 'a charming grotto of shells most tastefully arranged by Mrs Petrie Waugh and her two daughters.' The majority of these ornamentations appear to have gone, but there remains a gazebo, a circular building which is built into the wall of the Italian garden. Open on the garden side, it has three glazed windows through which to gaze at the sea from the bench curving round its interior wall. Restored in 1999, it sports a ball finial on an ogee roof and has a *clairvoyée*, or unglazed window, in the wall which curves down from the gazebo. Its builder is unknown but it is likely to date from the time of Waugh.

In the later nineteenth and early twentieth centuries Brownsea Castle, if not the whole island, was the playground of the rich. The *belle époque* was between 1901 and 1925 when Charles and Florence van Raalte, who were of Dutch extraction, owned the island, and it is clear from contemporary photographs that it was the scene of many glamorous parties and informal gatherings of European crowned heads. It is also clear that the gardens were a treasure trove of ornamentation: one wonders, for example, whatever happened to the enormous Ionic column that stood on the lawn of the Italian garden.

CHARBOROUGH PARK
(TOWER: OS REF: 195 SY 929 975; OTHERS NEARBY)

Long high walls are not a common feature of the county's estates, but Charborough Park is an exception. The wall's great length of some seven kilometres is broken by two magnificent entrances and one lodge, foretastes of the house which lies about a mile inside the wall. The gates were contemporary with a turnpike scheme that drove John Drax (1800-1887) close to bankruptcy in 1843, so determined was he to route the new road away from the house.

The Lion Gate is the first entrance visible going westwards along the A31. It has eight free-standing Ionic columns arranged in pairs, supporting a stucco-faced entablature and a platform from which a lion passant gazes out. The cast iron gates beneath were thought ornate enough to be exhibited at the Great Exhibition of 1862.

The next gate to the west and situated on a bend is the Stag Gate. It is made of Flemish bond brick with stone dressings, there is a high round-headed arch flanked by colossal square piers, and on top of a plain podium is the fine figure of a stag. The other lodges are less imperious, being East Almer Lodge at the west end of the estate by the road, and the Peacock Lodge, a classical building inside the estate half a mile from the main house. On East Almer Lodge John Drax first congratulated himself for building the new turnpike road on one

The Stag Gate, Charborough Park.

plaque and then celebrated his victory over another local landowner on a second: 'This road [through the park] was closed by order of the Magistrates, which was appealed against by James John Farquharson Esq. at the Epiphany Quarter Sessions held at Dorchester Janry 4th 1841 and after a trial of three days the order was confirmed by the order of Twelve Honest Jurymen.'

John Drax's most visible legacy is Charborough Tower, built originally by Edward Drax in 1790 to a height of eighty feet, probably for viewing his deer and possibly the sea. After it was struck by lightning in 1838, the octagonal tower was partly demolished by John

Drax who, not to be outdone, increased its height to 120 feet, an event recorded on yet another plaque:

THIS TOWER WAS BUILT BY EDWARD DRAX, ESQUIRE, IN THE YEAR 1790, DURING THE SHORT TIME HE WAS THE POSSESSOR OF CHARBOROUGH. IT WAS STRUCK BY LIGHTNING ON THE 29TH NOVEMBER 1838, WHICH SO DAMAGED IT THAT IT BECAME NECESSARY TO TAKE DOWN THE GREATER PART. IT WAS REBUILT IN 1839 BY JOHN SAMUEL WANLEY SAWBRIDGE ERLE DRAX ESQUIRE WHO CARRIED IT FORTY FEET HIGHER THAN IT WAS ORIGINALLY BUILT, MAKING THE PRESENT HEIGHT UPWARD OF ONE HUNDRED FEET

The five-storey tower has certainly survived better than many of the same era, although it has lost a couple of the pinnacles which protrude from the first floor level, and it leans slightly to the south. With a solid stone geometric open-well staircase, complete with iron balustrades, its Strawberry Hill Gothic style is complemented by the grotesque bearded head of a man on the banister rail inside the entrance. Except for the top floor, the windows are all blind and surrounded by the carved stone heads of monkeys, devils, bears and priests. The approach from the house to the tower is magnificent, up a long grassy avenue, a bridge and then a series of steps. The views from the top of the tower are superb; on a clear day four counties and the Isle of Wight are visible.

Charborough Tower was too prominent to escape the notice of Thomas Hardy, and it seems likely that it inspired *Two on a Tower*. Hardy gives the tower a Tuscan column not to be found on the real thing, whilst retaining the viewing platform from which the hero Swithin St Cleeve observes the stars. The description of the surrounding landscape suggests a location miles away from 'Welland House' - Hardy's name for Charborough House - where his heroine Lady Viviette Constantine lives, and he later wrote that he had in mind the tower at Horton as well as at Charborough. In the novel he places

Opposite The 120 foot high tower at Charborough Park, rebuilt to its present height by John Drax in 1839.

the tower on the ancient fortified hill of Weatherby Castle or 'Ring's-Hill Speer' near Milborne St Andrew, a few miles to the north-west of Charborough. The various movements of the heroine suggest that Hardy situated the novel around the tall obelisk on this hill (see page 54).

Charborough's main claim to fame is as the birthplace of the plot to depose James II, the so-called Glorious Revolution. The site of this intrigue is the Grove Icehouse, which has a tablet commemorating the event set above the door, and which attempts to accord to King William III more honours than he is due, exhorting us to maintain the good work done by the Dutchman:

UNDER THIS ROOF, IN THE YEAR MDCLXXXVI, A SET OF PATRIOTIC GENTLEMEN OF THIS NEIGHBOURHOOD CONCERTED THE GREAT PLAN OF THE GLORIOUS REVOLUTION WITH THE IMMORTAL KING WILLIAM; TO WHOM WE OWE OUR DELIVERANCE FROM POPERY AND SLAVERY, AND THE EXPULSION OF THE TYRANT RACE OF THE STUARTS THE RESTORATION OF OUR LIBERTY, THE SECURITY OF OUR PROPERTY, AND THE ESTABLISHMENT OF NATIONAL HONOUR. ENGLISHMEN, REMEMBER THIS GLORIOUS AREA, AND CONSIDER THAT YOUR LIBERTIES PROCURED BY THE VERTUES OF YOUR ANCESTERS, MUST BE MAINTAINED BY YOURSELVES.

The only slight disappointment is that the icehouse we see today is not the one in which the plot was hatched, but a late eighteenth century replacement, which itself later had an impressive mid-nineteenth century façade added. It is surmounted by a statue of Mercury copied from the Villa Medici in Rome, and has large urns on either side. Inside there is a small lobby and at the inner end of this ante-chamber is a nail-studded door with strap hinges which opens onto a passageway which leads to the ice chamber. Some twelve feet in diameter and sixteen feet from floor to spring of vault, the chamber is lined with narrow bricks and has a domed roof with a square trap covered by a metal grate.

John Drax went on to build the Byzantine Mausoleum at Holnest near Sherborne, a building which confirms his eccentricity. After the death of his wife, he went to live at Holnest Lodge, where he first

John Drax's extraordinary Byzantine Mausoleum in the churchyard at
Holnest before its demolition in 1935.

placed plaster statues of deities along the drive. His most grandiose
folly was the erection of a Column with lions at its foot *à la* Nelson,
and topped by a bronze statue of himself in a frock coat and holding
a silk hat. As for the mausoleum, he was to be its sole occupant. He
completed it in the adjacent churchyard at a cost of nearly £10,000
twenty-nine years before his death. Supposedly in the Byzantine style,
it was embellished with marble pillars, the door was covered in
bronze, and a heavy bronze Romanesque sarcophagus was placed in
the centre above the ground. There were twelve stained glass windows
depicting cardinal virtues such as Faith, Hope and Charity, as well as
a mosaic of a lady draped in coloured gauze garments poised on a
diaphanous cloud as if rising in flight. The building was barrel-
vaulted, with rich carvings in the portal, and a series of columns were
set into the walls.

Despite his good taste, John Drax was evidently afflicted not only
by *folie de grandeur* but also a morbid obsession with death, for he
rehearsed his own funeral. After lying down in an oak and lead-lined

coffin, his servants carried him to the churchyard, while Drax chastized them for every jolt. He also sent the coffin back to its makers in Sherborne, saying that it was too narrow for his shoulders. Fearful of the dark, Drax preferred to sleep during daylight, and at night he employed a watchman to circle the house and call out regularly 'All's Well!'.

When Drax finally died on the day before his eighty-seventh birthday, those who flocked to his real funeral did so not so much to pay their respects as to claim their legacy, for in his will Drax had promised that: 'there will be a sovereign for everyone who attends my funeral'. One can imagine the response on being told by the executors of Drax's estate that they already had a sovereign – 'she's on the throne!'. The Byzantine Mausoleum was demolished after falling into decay in 1935, a fate shared by the Nelson-like column and its adjacent statues.

COMPTON ACRES
(OS REF: 195 SZ 053 895)

Shortly after the First World War the financier Thomas Simpson bought a house overlooking Poole Harbour in Canford Cliffs, on the heathland typical of the eastern end of the county. Over the next thirty years he slowly realised his dream of creating a series of self-contained gardens, either on national themes or with a particular plant dominant, all of them almost theatrical in the way that they took advantage of the landscape's natural undulations. As Simpson's initial planting began to mature, there evolved the Italian Garden, the Woodland Walk and Sub-Tropical Glen, the Rock & Water Garden and the Heather Dell. The charm of Compton Acres is that it becomes a series of surprises, with each turn revealing a different style.

For the lover of the exotic none is more entrancing than the Japanese Garden. Here Simpson's passion for authenticity meant that the entire garden was built with imported Japanese stones and ornaments, designed by a Japanese architect and built by Japanese workmen. The garden is rich in oriental plants, many of them laden with symbolism, which mingle with small stone pagodas and bronze cranes. An air of sanctity is imposed at the entrance by a well for

The Imperial Red Teahouse in the Japanese Garden at Compton Acres,
Canford Cliffs.

The temple to Bacchus at Compton Acres.

washing one's feet out of respect for one's ancestors. Water is the predominant feature in the design. Thus the 'God of Punishment' is placed to keep away evil spirits which fear water and therefore cannot reach the Imperial Red Teahouse, only accessible across stepping stones placed in the pond. The small wooden building has wide eaves, each curving up at the corners into the shape of a bird's head, and is striking in its colour as it nestles in the greenery. The only room is small and simply arranged with a wicker chair and two slender occasional tables in the corners. The other buildings in the Japanese Garden are two rustic huts; a wooden and thatched summerhouse guarded by lions, and a wisteria covered Sewing Bower.

After the death of Simpson, Compton Acres was purchased by the London architect J.S. Beard, who restored the gardens from the decay into which they had fallen during the Second World War. From 1950 he embellished the estate, adding the herbaceous borders and in 1955, the Roman Garden, a circular paved court with statues and urns on plinths. It contains a pedimented portico and fine wrought iron gates opening into a simple grotto consisting of a short tunnel, open at both ends.

CREECH
(OS REF: 195 SY 912 817)

The fanciful building known as either Creech Arch, Grange Arch or Bond's Folly has been cared for by the National Trust since 1942 and enjoys excellent views over the Purbeck Hills to Poole Harbour. Sadly, it is not high enough on Ridgeway Hill to catch a view of the English Channel. Perhaps to have built it further would have obscured it from Creech Grange, the principal vantage from which it was intended to be admired.

An avenue of conifers was planted to lead the eye from the Grange bowling green up the steep slope of the hill to the three-arched structure, a vista long ago obscured by the growth of the Great Wood. The builder of the arch was Denis Bond, owner of Creech Grange and an MP for Poole, who died in the same year as its construction in 1746, and who gave London's Bond Street its name.

This positioning of buildings was a common landscape device,

Creech Arch, built by Denis Bond in 1746 and intended to be mistaken for an ancient castle when viewed from Creech Grange.

made into a conceit by the fact that many were deliberately built as ruins, often to instill an air of antiquity to an estate which may have only recently been developed. In the case of Creech, as in other country estates, the idea was to give the impression that on top of the hill there was an ancient castle, only a fragment of which was the arch, and from where the owner of the estate had moved into a more modern house.

Here the arch has indeed some of the air of a castle gateway, with an embattled parapet above the central arch and a plainer parapet above the side arches. The walls carry on to the side of the arches, and contain niches for sitting, as well as four pinnacles in the form of pyramids placed on the coping.

Lilian Bond, a descendant of Denis Bond, wrote in 1961 that she could also remember a 'temple', which was used as a summerhouse and was once one of several architectural delights around Creech Grange: 'It had fallen into decay or been removed before I could remember it, but the foundation stones are still there today. Some of the columns were made use of for supporting the verandah of the house at Stockford where my brother Walter lived in later years.'

In the parish of Buckland Newton there once stood an imposing Palladian house called Castle Hill, also known as Duntish Court, which was of sufficient importance to be illustrated in the influential architectural pattern book *Vitruvius Britannicus* (1771). It was built for Fitzwalter Foy in about 1760 by the renowned orientalist Sir William Chambers (1723-1796), architect to Kings George III and IV and responsible for the Chinese pagoda in Kew Gardens. The house soon fell into such decay that one owner set fire to it in order to avoid keeping up the pretence that it could be maintained, and on its site a single storey house was built in the twentieth century.

Castle Hill was not immune to the fashionable eighteenth century trend for 'improving' one's estates. The remaining features include a ruined summer-house, a statue of Diana, and a long pond surrounded by trees and shrubs. Close to one end of the pond are the remains of a small grotto. It is built mainly of freestone, a type of precipitated limestone, as well as red brick, gypsum and red calcite. Flints jut out from the wall, and it looks as if stalactites have broken off from the ceiling, along with other masonry. Like many grottoes, water is much in evidence, and here it is collected in small pools from a spring.

The remains of the grotto, Duntish Court.

ENCOMBE

The estate of Encombe enjoys one of the most unspoilt and dramatic locations in the Isle of Purbeck, tucked into a combe running down to the sea and accessible only from the village of Kingston and the Dorset Coastal Path.

John Pitt bought the estate in 1734 and proceeded to build a house slightly in the Vanbrugh style. If the house is too clumsy to bear the signature of the master of the English baroque, then the landscape is breathtaking. Pitt's second cousin William Pitt, the politician and 1st Earl of Chatham, described the estate as 'dear, unknown, delightful, picturesque Encombe', even though he never visited it. As William became more influential, so John profited too, becoming sufficiently wealthy to take advantage of the natural combe to create two lakes deliberately placed so as to make the house appear to be connected by an estuary to the sea. The trees have grown high enough to fudge such an illusion, but Pitt created one of the most significant examples of landscape art in Dorset.

John's son, William Morton Pitt, could not maintain the property, partly due to the extravagance of his wife, and so he sold Encombe to John Scott, 1st Earl of Eldon and a Lord Chancellor. Scott owed his

The Temple, Encombe.

A sea mist swirling round the 40 foot high obelisk above Encombe built in 1835 by John Scott, 1st Earl of Eldon, in memory of his brother, Sir William Scott, Baron Stowell.

fortune to the then legal profits of the plunder system, whereby money was seized from bankruptcies, lunacies and wardships, and some of which he spent on constructing a number of interesting features around the estate. One of these was the 'Temple', a fairly plain Tuscan building close to the house with two free-standing and two attached columns supporting a simple entablature and a higher than average pediment.

Far above the house is the 40-feet high obelisk (OS REF: 195 SY 947 790) commemorating his brother Sir William Scott, Baron Stowell. It stands high on a bluff with a view of the sea, is made of Seacombe limestone and its first stone was laid by John Scott's younger daughter

A drawing of the Rock Bridge, Encombe.

Lady Frances Bankes, who had married into one of the other great Dorset landowning families. Also in 1835 he had built the Eldon Seat (OS REF: 195 SY 937 778), a large stone vantage point looking out to sea, near to which a memorial stone to Eldon's dog Pincher was put up in 1840.

Eldon may not have built the Rock Bridge or Rock Arch (OS REF: 195 SY 945 782), but rather his predecessor William Morton Pitt - though little is certain. A painting of the house may hold the answer, for it includes men wearing tricorn hats which went out of fashion in the 1780s, whilst the bridge itself bears a resemblance to the one built in 1763 at Park Place, Henley-on-Thames. It not only carries the road leading to the south of the house over a stream but was also intended as an 'incident' on the circuit around the upper lake. This picturesque quality is created by its massive Purbeck Stone boulders and monolithic blocks set vertically, the latter giving it an imposing silhouette. Despite being functional, its effect is indisputably that of a grotto. There are three openings on the lower side, one of which contains nothing more than a stone bench, placed there for admiring a small fish pond, now gone, and the view of the lower lake and the sea, now both obscured by trees. As the Rock Bridge stood between two lakes intended to resemble an estuary, it is likely that the water level was higher when it was built, but now only a stream rushes through a channel beneath.

Sturt's Folly, better known as Horton Tower, is probably the first significant non-ecclesiastical tower to have been built in the county. Named 'Horton Observatory' on Taylor's map of Dorset of 1765, it stands 140 feet and seven storeys high and is the tallest folly in the county. It was built in about 1726 by Humphrey Sturt the Elder, possibly to the designs of Thomas Archer, and probably so that Sturt could follow the hunt when he became too old to ride in it; though it might also have been used as an astronomical observatory.

Thomas Archer lived twelve miles from Horton at Hale Park from 1715 to 1743. His sister-in-law was one of the Chafyn family, owners of nearby Chettle House, which he designed and whose rounded corners are duplicated in Horton Tower. Furthermore, Archer was one of the few English Baroque architects accustomed to building to a triangular groundplan, witnessed by his now demolished Rectory of St Paul's Church, Deptford, and his magnificent garden pavilion, well preserved at Wrest Park in Bedfordshire.

Gibbon, author of *The Decline and Fall of the Roman Empire*, wrote of Sturt; 'Such is the character of the man that he keeps his place in no order, sells his fish and makes a granary of his turret.' The 'turret' itself is truly a colossus. Almost unrelieved in red Flemish bond brick, on the inside it is a hexagon all the way up, with rooms leading off three of the sides, thus making it a triangle on the outside for the first five floors. These corner rooms end vertically in turrets topped by domes with ball finials, and act as a clever architectural device to make the transition easier to the two final storeys, which are hexagonal on the outside as well as the inside. There may have been a gigantic ogee-curved cupola with an open lantern on the very top, possibly, like Swithin St Cleeve in Hardy's *Two on a Tower*, for Sturt to look at the heavens.

Despite Sturt's improvements to the estate, including a large artificial lake, the tower may never have been completed, and his son Humphrey Sturt the Younger turned the lake back into meadow when he married into the Napier family of Crichel and made Crichel House his home. For many years the whole building was a wrecked shell with all the floors collapsed and only the remains of the internal

The drawing of Horton Tower on Isaac Taylor's 1765 map of Dorset.
Compare this view with the photograph of Horton Tower
on the front cover.

fireplaces showing where each storey started. The crumbling fabric was long of concern to its owners, English Heritage, and in 1992 the building was strengthened and repaired prior to Racal Vodaphone installing mobile telephone transmitter equipment at the top. Other restoration included a new roof, albeit not domed as before but flat, panes of glass in the windows on the top two floors and black-painted wooden blind windows on floors one to four, while the ground floor remains windowless as always.

KIMMERIDGE
(OS REF: 195 SY 908 786)

Overlooking the sea at Kimmeridge Bay is one of the most dramatically placed of all follies in Dorset, the Clavel Tower. It was built in about 1820 by the Reverend John Richards, who took the name Clavel from the previous owners of nearby Smedmore House on

A distant view of the Clavel Tower, Kimmeridge, showing how close it is to the edge of the cliff.

inheriting the estate in 1817. It may have been intended as an eyecatcher from the house, but like the Creech Arch any such vista has long been obscured by trees. As for Clavel, he never married, preferring Smedmore and the solitude of the tower, where he was warmed by fireplaces on each floor until his death in 1833.

The predominant colour of the stone is a reddish brown, though it briefly changed colour in the 1980s for the filming of the television series 'The Black Tower', based on the novel by crime writer P.D. James. Television technicians painted the tower with a black vegetable dye which they hoped would eventually be washed out by the weather. In the event, the dye obstinately refused to fade, and a steam-cleaning company was hired to return the tower to its normal colour.

The history of the tower has not been a happy one. As early as 1906, Frederick Treves wrote it off as a 'ridiculous tower' in *Highways and Byways in Dorset*. Perhaps what offended him about this circular tower of brick and stone was the mixture of architectural styles contained in three stories and a semi-basement, with Gothic window openings and handrail around the top, and a Doric colonnade encircling the ground floor. Some of the windows have been blocked up, the remains of the staircase on the outside are barely visible and the parapet once boasted quatrefoil openings.

Clavel Tower, Kimmeridge.

As I wrote in the introduction to this book, Clavel Tower faces the most uncertain future of all Dorset's follies. Salt-laden winds and winter storms have slowly eroded the cliff on which it stands, and unless something is done to stabilise the cliff it is only a matter of time before the entire tower tumbles into the sea.

The Bankes family first acquired their vast Dorset estates in 1635 when Sir John Bankes, then Charles I's Attorney General, purchased Corfe Castle, thus founding a dynasty that came to own much of the land in the east of the county. Among the family's properties was Kingston Lacy, once owned by John of Gaunt, and where in the fifteenth century the Duke of Somerset had built a manor house. It was here, on a nearby site, that following the Restoration of Charles II in 1660 Sir John's son, Ralph, commissioned Sir Roger Pratt to build Kingston Lacy House. In 1835 Pratt's red brick walls were faced with ashlar by Sir Charles Barry, so what we see today is a vaguely classical house, but without the columns one might expect in a house of the period.

The impetus for the alterations came from the then owner of Kingston Lacy, William Bankes, an inveterate traveller who spent eight years wandering around Italy, the eastern Mediterranean and the Middle East, and who in later life was obliged to leave England permanently to escape conviction for homosexuality. His sharp but extravagant personality appealed to many, including Lord Byron, who nicknamed him 'the father of all mischiefs'. Despite his dissolute nature, Bankes was a great connoisseur and collector, and although exiled from England, filled Kingston Lacy with works by the likes of Veronese, Guido Reni, Raphael, Velaquez and Murillo.

William Bankes also left his mark as an Egyptologist, for he played a minor part in the interpretation of Egyptian hieroglyphics, in which the Rosetta Stone was also a key element. Bankes' contribution to the unravelling of the linguistic riddle was the recording of the hieroglyphics and Greek inscription on the Philae Needle, one of two pink granite obelisks which stood in front of the temple of Isis on the island of Philae. Bankes first saw the obelisk in 1815, but its transportation to England was marred by many mishaps, including falling into the Nile, and its re-erection on the lawns at Kingston Lacy was not finally completed until 1839.

The obelisk's removal from Egypt was entrusted to Giovanni Belzoni, a one-time strongman who abandoned his theatrical career as the 'Patagonian Sampson' in favour of that of an hydraulics engineer

The Egyptian obelisk on the lawn at Kingston Lacy.

and excavator of Egyptian antiquities. The Duke of Wellington lent a gun carriage to transport it to Kingston Lacy, and laid its foundation stone.

The hieroglyphics on the obelisk date from the reign of Ptolemy Euergetes (died 116 BC) and record the exemption of the priests of Isis from bearing the expenses of the local administration. Bankes added an inscription to the base, which reads:

'William John Bankes Esq M.P. caused this obelisk to be removed and the pedestal from which it had fallen to be removed under the direction of G. Belzoni in 1819 from the island of Philae beyond the first cataract and brought this platform - the stepped base from the nuns of Hierassycaminon in Nubia. The granite used in the preparation of this monument was brought from the remains of Leptis Magna in Africa and was given for that purpose by His Majesty King George IV.'

William was not the first of the family to erect an obelisk. In a letter written by his father, Henry, when the bricks for another obelisk's foundations were piled opposite his window, he described

The survivor of a pair of obelisks in Upper Park, Kingston Lacy, built by John Bankes in the 1730s.

their appetite for follies as 'a disorder in the Bankes family, which sometimes passes over one generation, like madness or gout, or the king's evil, and breaks out again in the next; my uncle. . . could not help erecting two Obelisks' and thought his uncle had built enough.

Henry was referring to John Bankes the Younger's erection of two relatively small obelisks in Upper Park, a field to the south of the house. One of these has gone, but the survivor stands at what was probably the end of a diagonal axis opened up by uprooting elms to create a vista in 1734-5.

A third surviving obelisk can be found in the fernery to the east of the house, and was erected by Walter Ralph Bankes to commemorate Queen Victoria's Golden Jubilee in 1887. All three obelisks can be seen from each other as well as the house, and visiting them makes an agreeable circuit around the grounds. The estate was bequeathed by Ralph Bankes to the National Trust in 1981.

KINGSTON MAURWARD
(OS REF: 194 SY 715 909)

The estate takes its name from the Maurward family, who were the ancient lords of the area. Later, it was acquired through marriage by the Greys, who built the original manor house in the late sixteenth century, standing to the east of the estate. Following the marriage of Laura, the last Grey heiress, the manor house became a farmhouse, and a new family seat, Kingston Maurward House was built a little to the west between 1717 and 1720. Laura's husband George Pitt of Stratfield Saye in Hampshire, the cousin of Prime Minister William Pitt the Elder, was responsible for its construction, and in 1794 George Pitt's great nephew, William Morton Pitt, encased the house in Portland stone as a result of a remark by George III who said that he did not like red brick houses. The result is a fine three-storeyed house with pediments, pilasters and sash windows, described by Hutchins as an 'elegant and stately pile' which 'makes a grand figure.'

William Morton Pitt and his father John Pitt also owned Encombe (see page 31) where they may have been responsible for the rock arch that carries the road over it and doubles as a grotto. It was John Pitt who first developed the grounds at Kingston Maurward, forming a

The Lakeside Temple, Kingston Maurward.

lake complete with islands out of a number of canals and pieces of water. He held Kingston Maurward from 1774 to 1787, during which time he also erected the Lakeside Temple, a Grecian-style summerhouse of brick faced with Portland stone. The building does not have much of an interior, if at all, for the double doors have no handle and there are no windows. Instead, there is a raised patio sheltered by a portico of four Doric columns, approached up a flight of five steps. The entablature of the portico is pedimented unremarkably but the curving screen walls on either side are finished with unusually wide capitals, as well as bare niches.

We may never know if they contained any statues, nor if any divine creature graced the bare plinth in the middle of the pond just in front of the temple. Its siting is good in respect of the adjacent lake and the main house, but is marred by the line of student accommodation blocks just behind the temple, deriving from the estate's new role as the Kingston Maurward Agricultural College.

Before its current use, the estate passed through one final glorious age when it was owned by the Hanbury family. At its head was Sir Cecil Hanbury, who became MP for North Dorset and did good works in the county. Sir Cecil had acquired his wealth mainly through the Shanghai Silkworks and Waterworks and put it to good use in embellishing the house and grounds. He preferred the life of a Dorset landowner to that of an oriental trader, entertaining royalty and politicians as well as literary figures, including Thomas Hardy, with whom he was especially friendly.

It was Dodo, Sir Cecil's wife, who was behind many of the developments in the gardens, and she instigated the laying out of the Armistice Walk by the lake and the formal gardens to the west of the house. Among the improvements was The Temple of the Four Winds, a rotunda built on a mound used two centuries earlier for surveying the construction of the Georgian House. The temple was removed in 1938 by Dodo after the death of Sir Cecil to their property at La Mortola on the Italian Riviera, the Villa Hanbury, which is remarkable for its terraced gardens. The mound stood bare for over fifty years until 1995 when it was replaced by a similar temple, giving fine views over the various themed gardens of the estate.

The Temple of the Four Winds, Kingston Maurward, built by students at Weymouth College in 1995 to replace a similar temple that had been taken to Italy in 1938.

The present temple was reconstructed in Portland stone by Weymouth College masonry students working from original drawings and acts as a memorial to Ralph Fitzau (1908-1983), a dealer in goat skins and products and a friend of a former vice-principal of the college. Judging from the inscriptions to be found on the temple, Fitzau was sorely missed by his wife Jenny. The inscription on the plinth of one of the columns says '*Vous et Nul Autre*', (old French for 'You and None Other'), whilst that on the inside of the entablature in part lists the places that the Fitzaus either lived in or visited 'LOVE TRANSCENDS TIME AND PLACE: PRUSSIA, GERMANY, SWITZERLAND, PAKISTAN, INDIA, ENGLAND'. At the centre of the marble floor, inset in engraved stones in a concentric pattern, is the date 1631 and the coat-of-arms of the Fitzau family, depicting a warrior on horseback brandishing a sword. Above is the finest of wrought iron cupolas rising to a weathervane. Here the original differs from the latest version of the temple, in that the former has a hollow shape of a lion rampant, and the latter the silhouette of a dog.

LILLINGTON
(OS REF: 195 ST 633 123)

On a slight rise to the east of the village of Lillington stands an octagonal water tower about 70 feet high, and which was designed in about 1930 by Maxwell Ayston. Despite the water tower's proximity to the house that was eventually to become St Anthony's-Leweston School, it did not supply water to the house, but to the village in the days before it was connected to the mains.

The tower has three levels of slit windows and an outside wooden staircase leading to a belvedere room with large-paned windows and a conical copper roof from which to admire the surrounding countryside. Faintly Art Deco in design, in 2000 it was being restored and converted into a holiday home with seven levels by the Saxon architectural practice.

Opposite The 1930s water tower at Lillington, near Sherborne, photographed in the spring of 2000 when in the process of being converted into a house.

LULWORTH

The estate at Lulworth has a number of conceits which tease the beholder into believing that they are something else. Here we are in Weld country, one of the county's most important landowners, and Roman Catholics for generations, producing a cardinal and the founder of Stonyhurst, the public school. The castle was built from 1608, and was described in *The Architecture of Southern England* as 'never really a castle at all but a vast Jacobean folly'. A massive square bulk with circular towers on each corner, it has recently been restored by English Heritage after being gutted by fire in 1929.

Thanks to his friendship with George III, who was accustomed to take the waters in nearby Weymouth, in 1795 Thomas Weld was granted permission to build the first Roman Catholic church in England since the Reformation. The condition was that it had to be built in the form of a garden temple, though with its faintly Palladian quatrefoil-plan it in fact looks more like a mausoleum. It was designed by John Tasker, who was also responsible for the redecoration of the castle's interior in the Adam style between 1780 and 1782.

The church at Lulworth Castle, started in 1795 by Thomas Weld and the first Catholic church to be built in England since the Reformation.

The Wareham Gate Lodge, Lulworth Castle.

Thomas Weld was also responsible for most of the other buildings in the park, including a number of gate lodges. Firstly, on the western boundary of the estate, there are the Clare Towers (OS REF: 194 SY 842 830) which date from about 1796 and were probably the work of John Tasker. The gateway consists of an archway flanked by round towers about 6 feet in diameter and 18 feet high. Named after Clare Arundell, who married Humphrey Weld in 1641, the gateway is substantially decayed.

In better condition is the Wareham Gate Lodge (OS REF: 194 SY 857 827) at the eastern end of the estate, and which dates from the seventeenth century. It appears in Thomas Weld's notebooks in 1806 as a 'Design for introducing the Old Lodge which stood in front of the Castle until the year 1753' and appears again in a drawing of 1721, showing that it gave access to a formal garden. It lay in a heap of stones for over half a century until it was re-erected in 1808 on its present site on the East Lulworth to Coombe Keynes road, where a stone in the façade reveals the date of its removal. It is a rectangular two-storey building with a high parapet with crenellations, and a carriageway runs through the middle.

The North, or Triangular, Lodges, Lulworth Castle, which now
stand in the middle of open country.

Of greater originality are the North Lodges, or Triangular Lodges
(OS REF: 194 SY 848 833), a pair of small three-sided buildings at the
Coombe Keynes end of the estate. Rounded at the corners and topped
by crenellations, these two-storey towers stand about forty feet apart
but are connected by arches, each with its own gate for pedestrians,
gate piers and an elegant carriage gate. The gate piers contain, on the
south side, a niche and oval panels framing the date 1785. On the
north side there is a demonstration of firstly, unity in the form of a
shield of arms showing Weld quartering Sherborne, Heveningham and
Simeon, and secondly, rivalry, showing Weld impaling Stanley. Lions
couchant complete the imperiousness of the piers. Extending either
side of the lodges is a decaying park wall made of brown carstone with
the remains of three small towers with castellations, varying in height
up to about 12 feet.

Sadly, all three gateways have virtually ceased to perform the
function they were originally built for. All are approached along
muddy or grassy tracks, except the Wareham Gate Lodge which is
hard by the public road, but even there the drive leads to little more
than a hut set by a clearing in the woods.

Of equal redundancy is the Fort on the Lake (OS REF: 194 SY 861
839). The first question any student of landscape design would ask
would be how the lake relates to the central features of the Lulworth

The Fort on the Lake, built by Joseph Weld in 1851 to house a model brig. The lake was formed in 1837 to test model boats for the Admiralty.

estate, as it does not seem to form part of a landscape plan. The answer is unexpected and unusual: the lake was created in 1837 for the purpose of testing model boats for the Admiralty. Finally, Joseph Weld built the fort in about 1851 to house a model brig of his own design, sadly destroyed by souvenir hunters in the Second World War.

The fort itself still stands, like a gazebo on a platform projecting into the lake, circular and battlemented and made of rubble with brick dressings. Approached from the land through an archway with iron gates, there used to be cannons poking out from the gaps in the platform wall, looking impregnable from this little sea, and completing the sham militaristic air.

MAPPERTON
(OS REF: 194 SY 503 995)

The Manor House at Mapperton is a very fine example of Tudor, Stuart and later architecture blended together with beautiful ochre Ham stone. It was mentioned in the Domesday Book, when it was

The late seventeenth century Pool House, Mapperton.

owned by William de Moion, a Sheriff of Somerset, since whose time it belonged to only four families until the twentieth century – the Bretts, Morgans, Brodrepps and Comptons. Despite the present house being built in several periods, firstly in 1550-60 by Robert Morgan, then in the 1660s by Richard Brodrepp, and finally in the eighteenth century, there is a great degree of homogeneity in style which belies the many additions and alterations. The most striking part is the west front with its E-plan, typical of the Elizabethan age, in fact mainly seventeenth century. In the centre there is a fine porch built by Brodrepp whose arms are fixed on the outer wall and whose initials 'R.B' and the date 1666 are scratched into the inside of the porch.

It is this date, or thereabouts, that is significant for the garden which nestles in the combe immediately to the east of the house. It was in the era of the restoration of Charles II that the Dutch style of garden enjoyed a brief fashion, and Mapperton is one of the very few places in Britain that it can still be seen. Another, more famous, example of the Dutch style is at Westbury Court in Gloucestershire, which has a tall pavilion as the focal point at end of one of two long canals bordered by continuous hedges. At Mapperton, the pool is much shorter and is bordered by several individual topiary hedges cut into rounded conical shapes, and there is much later planting which follows twentieth century fashion, thus making the scene more varied in style. Like at Westbury Court, the focal point at Mapperton is a tall pavilion, which is usually known as the Pool House, a two-storeyed building made of a Ham stone similar to that of the main house. Standing at the north end of the pool, the Pool House has an arched wooden door at ground level which opens into an interior of little note, but the upper chamber is more interesting. Wooden panelling covers the walls, a corner cupboard is attached to the join of two walls, and a fireplace is still serviceable and able to create a cosy atmosphere for the likes of Ethel Labouchère. The widow of a banker, she was owner of the Mapperton from 1919 to 1955, and painted the delightful scene around her from behind the leaded windows overlooking the pool. On the outside, a solid chimney rises from the upper level, and an *akebia quintata* creeps up the stone which is becoming encrusted with white lichen, adding a texture of antiquity to what is one of the oldest garden buildings in Dorset.

The upper level of the Pool House cannot be reached directly from the interior of the lower level, but is approached by mounting a series of steps either side of the building and then walking along a terrace. This terrace is the start of the Italianate garden created by Ethel Labouchère in the 1920s, and which rivals the lower garden for

One of a pair of summer-houses, that face each-other across the Italian gardens created by Ethel Labouchère in the 1920s at Mapperton.

charm. There is much of interest to horticulturists in plants such as the wisteria and roses which twine themselves around the columns of a pergola which leads from the Pool House towards the centre piece, an octagonal pond sculpted with leaf motifs. There are classical statues scattered at intervals and at the north end of this garden stands the Orangery, used for the cultivation of plants such as lemon trees and built by the 10th Earl of Sandwich whose family started living at the property shortly after he purchased it in 1955

At the top of steps to either side of the pond, and facing each other, are what have been called grottoes, but without any of the shell-work, tufa, or running water which characterise the typical grotto. They are certainly an unusual type of summerhouse, set into the side walls of the garden and having a colonnade on the front and a single open chamber. Here the similarity ends, for the west summerhouse has gravel on the floor, a large curved niche at the back and several smaller ones elsewhere, along with small stands for placing lamps, and a small fireplace with a sculpted overmantel, while the east summerhouse has a paved floor, a large fireplace, two square niches and columns which support the ceiling. In these summerhouses too, it is said that Ethel Labouchère painted, and no doubt captured on canvas an enchanting scene.

One of the most ancient estates in Dorset, and still private, Melbury has a glorious park filled with a wide variety of mature trees. The house has its origins in the early fifteenth century, having been owned by the Bruning family from whom Henry Strangways acquired the estate through marriage in 1500. His son Sir Giles used 3,000 loads of Ham stone to erect one of the first prospect towers in England, a hexagon with a fine lantern with the aim of viewing the deer. When John Leland visited in 1540 he noted that 'Mr Strangeguayse hath now a late much buildid at Mylbyri quadrato, avauncing the inner part of the house with a loftie and fresch tower.' The tower fails to be a true folly because a house was built around it, and the front that we see today mainly dates from 1692, being in a provincial classical style, and elsewhere there are Tudor parts remaining.

One of these is the hexagonal Turret, or Garden House, which again was originally isolated but became subsumed by an extension of

The Tudor Garden House at Melbury.

the house. Of coursed rubble with ashlar dressings, it has eighteenth century gothic additions including pinnacles and an embattled parapet. The ogee ceiling is particularly attractive, with moulded angle ribs and a painted shield-of-arms. It may have been used as a dovecote or summerhouse for outdoor meals or entertainments, and now forms the corner of the wall of the eighteenth century kitchen garden.

The kitchen garden was created by Susannah Strangways Horner after she had embellished the house, and was one of a series of gardens laid out in the 1740s. A ha-ha was built to divide the garden from the deer park and the stream to the east was dammed to create ponds. The lake was originally smaller and more formal than what we see today, but by 1780 it had been extended into an irregular form to fit the contours of the land.

We cannot be sure whether it was Susannah or her daughter, the 1st Countess of Ilchester, who built the grotto, which stands just above the head of the lake and is fed by water channelled from a small pond. It is about 4 feet high, mound-shaped with rough, moss-covered stones forming the roof. There is a small opening on one side, and a bigger one on the other, out of which the water falls over haphazardly arranged stones to the lake below.

MILBORNE ST ANDREW
(OS REF: 194 SY 807 962)

The obelisk at Weatherby Castle, an Iron Age hillfort reduced to a raised earthwork, would have been more visible when it was built in 1761 by Edmund Morton Pleydell than it is today, with the wood grown up around it. Why he erected it remains uncertain, apart from being an eye-catcher from Milborne House, his home in Milborne St Andrew. What he left is a plain red brick shaft with a bronze globe at the top, making a height of 60 feet. For posterity he inscribed a plaque with 'E.M.P. 1761', since when the obelisk has slowly deteriorated. In 1990 it was made safe against falling debris. £2,000 was raised to stabilise its fabric, and a new black sham beehive was placed on the globe, around which crows now circle.

The obelisk is perhaps most interesting from a literary point-of-view, probably being the setting for the tower scenes in *Two on a*

Woodland now surrounds the obelisk on Weatherby Hill, Milborne St
Andrew, built by Edmund Morton Pleydell in 1761.

Tower, Thomas Hardy's tale of a married woman drawn into a
relationship with an astronomer who gazes at the stars from the top
of a tower (see earlier under Charborough).

A pen and wash drawing of the Sham Chapel, Milton Abbas.
The drawing, by an unknown architect, is of the original design
and probably dates from the early nineteenth century.

MILTON ABBAS
(OS REF: 194 ST 793 020)

Nestling in an unspoilt combe, Milton Abbey benefits from a superb position and a history which stretches back to the Middle Ages. The Sham Chapel was probably built to consolidate that air of antiquity. A neglected piece of landscape art, possibly to serve as an eyecatcher from the abbey, from where it would have been visible when first built, it is now almost surrounded by trees.

There is no certainty about who built it. It may have appeared as early as 1780 after Joseph Damer, Lord Milton, had demolished the old Milton Abbas village and built a new one in a 'model' pattern to the designs of Capability Brown and Sir William Chambers, the architect of the present mansion. A third contender is James Wyatt, who continued the work after Chambers resigned in 1774.

However, Pevsner is convinced that the Sham Chapel could not have been built before 1813, which would rule out all three. The

Looking up at the 75 foot high obelisk at Moreton
built in the 1780s as a memorial to James Frampton.

Department of the Environment's Listed Buildings Report also puts it
in the early nineteenth century, probably on stylistic grounds. If it did
have a style it has mostly crumbled away, notably a central raised
gable with battlemented parapet and an octagonal pinnacle with a
Latin cross on its top. A few gothic arches remain, and the chancel is
relatively intact, but the whole of the west side has disappeared and a
tree on another side is threatening to push down the wall. A pen and
ink drawing in the collection of the Royal Institute of British
Architects may well be of the original building: it has the same quaint
details on the truncated spire, although it shows only half of the front.

MORETON
(OS REF: 194 SY 807 884)

In the same way that the obelisk at Weatherby is obscured by trees, so
is the one at Moreton, despite being 75 feet (23m) high. Its summit is
a massive 10 feet high urn, below which is an impressive shaft of cut

stone. The obelisk was built by James Hamilton of Weymouth in 1785-86 for Captain John Houlton in memory of James Frampton, who died in 1784. Hamilton is better known for designing the monument to George III in Weymouth.

The Frampton family had held the manor of Moreton since the fourteenth century and the house we see today half a mile to the north was built by James Frampton earlier in the eighteenth century. Adjacent is the parish church whose lychgate walls carry tablets originally set into the fabric of the obelisk, and whose inscription reads:

'Erected by Capt. John Houlton as a public testimony of his gratitude And respect for James Frampton Esq of this place.'

PORTESHAM
(OS REF: 194 SY 613 875)

The largest folly in the west of the county is undoubtedly the Hardy Monument, which serves as a very visible reminder of Dorset's links with the sea and of one of the most glorious eras of Britain's naval supremacy, the Napoleonic Wars. The boy who was to become Vice-Admiral Sir Thomas Masterman Hardy was born in 1769, the second son of Nanny Masterman of Kingston Russell and Joseph Hardy of Portesham, where he lived until at the age of thirteen he entered the Royal Navy as a 'captain's servant'.

He first met the man with whom he will always be linked, Horatio Nelson, when in 1796 Nelson hoisted his Commodore's pennant on the frigate *Minerve* at Gibraltar, on which Hardy was a young lieutenant. Shortly afterwards, as the *Minerve* was being chased by the Spanish through the Straits of Gibraltar, a sailor fell overboard. Hardy had the jolly boat lowered, and set out to save him. The current carried him towards the leading Spaniard, making capture seem inevitable. At which point Nelson cried 'By God, I'll not lose Hardy! Back the mizen top-sail!' The Spaniard hesitated and shortened sail, enabling the jolly boat to reach the *Minerve* in safety.

In 1798, Nelson appointed Hardy his flag-captain on the *Vanguard*, forging a professional relationship that continued after both men transferred to the *Victory* and lasted until Nelson's death at

The Hardy Monument, built above Portesham in the 1840s as a memorial
to Admiral Sir Thomas Hardy, who was born in Portesham and was
Nelson's captain on board HMS *Victory* at the Battle of Trafalgar.

the Battle of Trafalgar in 1805. Hardy was by Nelson's side on the
quarter-deck when he was shot, and was with him in the cockpit when
the dying admiral spoke the words with which Hardy will always be
associated, 'Kiss Me, Hardy', providing the nickname which
distinguishes him from Dorset's other Thomas Hardy. By a quirk of
coincidence, the novelist was able to see the monument from his
birthplace cottage in Higher Bockhampton, and even attempted to
prove that they shared a common ancestry.

Hardy died in 1839, by which date he was a baronet, a vice-
admiral, and Governor of Greenwich Hospital. Construction of the
monument started five years later, with funding for the project coming
from a public subscription to build a memorial on what Lord Ilchester,

who proposed the project, called a 'conspicuous spot'. The site chosen was the beacon mound on land owned by Hardy's nephew, and was close to his home village of Portesham on Black Down or Blagdon Hill, where many years before he had erected a rick of furze faggots to serve as a landmark for sea-going craft. Now there was something more permanent in the form of a 72 feet (22m) tower of ashlar stone from his nephew's quarry at Luckham's Pond. Built by the contractor Henry Goddard of Bridport to the design of Arthur Dyke Troyte, it stands 780 feet (238m) above sea level, affording excellent views of the Dorset coast down to Portland and far to the east and west. The foundation stone was laid on 21st October 1844, the 39th anniversary of the Battle of Trafalgar, and despite subscriptions pouring in from all over the county, it was not completed until 1848 at a cost of £609 and 16 shillings. It has to be said that it is not elegant. It begins as a broad, sloping octagon, then after twenty or so feet rises vertically to a parapet that could once be reached by an internal staircase. The inscription above the doorway reads:

ERECTED BY PUBLIC SUBSCRIPTION IN THE YEAR 1844

IN MEMORY OF

VICE-ADMIRAL SIR THOMAS MASTERMAN HARDY

BART., G.C.B.

FLAG-CAPTAIN TO LORD NELSON

ON H.M.S. 'VICTORY' AT THE BATTLE OF TRAFALGAR

RESTORED 1900

AND PLACED IN CHARGE OF THE NATIONAL TRUST FOR PLACES

OF HISTORIC INTEREST OR NATURAL BEAUTY BY THE

DESCENDANTS OF SIR THOMAS MASTERMAN HARDY

ON WHOSE LAND IT STANDS

Hardy's reputation has faded with time, but even in the early twentieth century he was still regarded as a national hero, to the extent that in *Nelson's Hardy: His Life Letters and Friends*, the author was confident enough to say of Hardy that he 'needs no visible memorial to keep his memory green in the fair countryside from which he sprang. His name and exploits have become, as it were, part and parcel of the Wessex folklore.'

The estates at Sherborne date back to medieval times when the old castle, now ruined, was built. In the late sixteenth century, Sir Walter Raleigh built himself what became known as the 'new' castle situated across the valley to the south.

In the early eighteenth century the poet and landscape designer Alexander Pope visited Sherborne. He became friends with Robert Digby, son of William, the 5th Lord Digby, and the two maintained a lively correspondence which resulted in Digby visiting Pope's garden, with its unusual grotto tunnel, in Twickenham. It is probable that Pope had some influence on the landscaping at Sherborne, and when Robert Digby died at the age of 34 in 1726, Pope wrote the epitaph on his tomb in Sherborne Abbey.

As for Pope, he is commemorated by Pope's Seat, which is more of a niche built into the bank overlooking the lake, though whether he advised on its building we cannot be sure. A somewhat plain affair, it is painted red and white on its semi-circular back wall, and has crenellations on the top. Pope was struck by Sherborne enough to declare that its beauty 'arises from this Irregularity, for not only the several parts of the Garden itself make the better Contraste by these sudden Rises, Falls and Turns of ground; but the Views about it are let in, and hang over the Walls, in very different figures and aspects.'

Pope's Seat is just one resting place on the tour round the lake, a promenade likely to be increasingly enjoyed by the Digby's and their guests as the number of features grew. After Edward, the 6th Lord Digby, inherited the Sherborne estates at the age of 20 in 1752, he and his brothers showed an immediate interest in landscape design. In 1753 the valley between the old and new castles flooded. So delighted was Edward with the temporary lake, that he employed the rising young landscape gardener Lancelot 'Capability' Brown to make it more permanent. It is by no means certain that Brown had a hand in all of the smaller architectural features, though the frequency of his visits over a thirty year period may have meant that he saw many of them built. It seems likely that he had a say in the 'cascade', if only because it tumbles towards the lake which he created and which is dammed by a bank of stones.

The Sham Ruin in the park at Sherborne, built in 1756
and intended to be viewed from the New Castle.

A little way up from the 'cascade', and part of the perimeter wall,
is Raleigh's Seat, where the famous navigator and soldier was
supposed to have been drenched in water by a servant in an attempt
to extinguish a fuming pipe. Sir Walter Raleigh acquired Sherborne
Old Castle in 1592, and finding that little could be done to convert the
medieval castle, built what he called 'Sherborne Lodge' to distinguish
it from the Old Castle, though it has since become known as
Sherborne ('New') Castle.

We next encounter Pope's Seat, and then a couple of hundred
metres further on in open grassland, the Sham Ruin, which still serves
as an eyecatcher designed to be seen from the New Castle. It was built
by Daniel Penny, one of a family of local builders whose names
regularly appear in the estate accounts. In March 1756 Penny was
paid £22 15s 5d for 'building ruins under the Castle'. A year later the
accounts list a payment of £4 8s 6d 'for finishing the tower'.

The stone wall with mock crenellations which runs along the southern edge of Castle Hill, and closes the park off from the remains of Sherborne Old Castle, was probably built at about the same time, and is shown in an entry of £10 6s 6d in the account book for March 1755. It is possible that the Sham Ruin was sited in order to be mistaken by observers as a supposed adjunct to the Old Castle, which is quite close but outside the present perimeter of the landscape park. The folly consists simply of a semi-circular wall about sixteen feet high and designed to create a 'tower' look, with a few scattered windows. It then straightens out and gradually slopes to the ground in a rather tumbling, irregular structure of stone.

STALBRIDGE
(OS REF: 194: SY 807 962)

Sir James Thornhill (1675-1734) was born at Melcombe Regis and was the most successful and popular decorative painter of the early eighteenth century. He enjoyed the patronage of George I and his son George II, and among his most famous works are the interior of the dome of St Paul's Cathedral and the Painted Hall in the Royal Naval College, Greenwich. His surviving work in Dorset includes frescoes in Sherborne House and Charborough House (see page 20), as well as the altarpiece in St Mary's Church, Weymouth, where he was Member of Parliament from 1722 to 1734. Ten years later he was appointed one of the Commissioners responsible for rebuilding Blandford after the fire of 1731, designing a 'Town Hall, General Assembly, Market House etc'. Although Thornhill died before rebuilding began, the Town Hall has resemblances to his design.

Such was Thornhill's success that he was able to buy back one of his family seats near Stalbridge, where he rebuilt the house in the Palladian style, but incorporating features from the older house. The capital probably came from a judicious selling of South Sea Company stock before the bubble burst. Then in 1727, the year of the accession of George II, he erected a forty-feet high obelisk on a slight rise several hundred metres to the north of the house in honour of the new king, who was to become his patron, and his wife, Queen Caroline.

The shaft of the obelisk is quite plain, and is supported by a stepped pedestal with a moulded cornice. Both are made of Bath freestone, while the stone for the foundation came from the local quarries at Marnhull. On the pedestal is an inscription which at first sight suggests that the new monarch's European dominions included France, but this was a conventional title of the time, and not intended to be flattering:

IN HON. DOM. AVGVSTAE
V. ID. V. OCTOB. C|Ɔ DCCXXVII
DIE INAVGVRANDIS SS. PP.
GEORGIO II: ET CAROLINAE
MAG. BRITAN FRAN. ET HIBERN
R. ET R. SOLENNITER DICATO
IACOBUS THORNHILL EQUES
D.S.   P.C.

'D.S.' stands for 'de suo' and 'P.C.' is short for 'ponendum curavit'. The whole inscription can be translated as:

IN HONOUR OF THE AUGUST HOUSE
ON 11TH OCTOBER 1727
THE DAY OF THE CORONATION OF THEIR MOST SERENE
MAJESTIES
GEORGE II AND CAROLINE
OF GREAT BRITAIN, FRANCE AND IRELAND
KING AND QUEEN, THIS WAS MOST SOLEMNLY DEDICATED
BY SIR JAMES THORNHILL
WHO FROM HIS OWN RESOURCES ARRANGED FOR IT TO BE
ERECTED

The obelisk is protected by black-painted railings with particularly arresting braces to strengthen them against the livestock grazing in the surrounding field. The original obelisk was demolished in a gale in 1836 and what we see today is a reconstruction, which may incorporate some of the original stone, but whose proportions are different, suggesting that much of the stone is new. Certainly the top is very different from the original, and we know that the inscription comes from the time of the rebuilding because a broken fragment of the original obelisk is preserved in the staircase in Thornhill House.

Sir James Thornhill's original drawing of the obelisk he built above his house near Stalbridge in honour of George II and Queen Caroline.

Few individual men or women have left their imprint on one town to the extent that George Burt did on Swanage. The features he erected are a testament to a philanthropic vision inspired by a wish to improve his home town. Nowadays it is hard to ignore his legacy in this pleasant resort on the Purbeck coast, which has been described as 'Old London by the Sea'. Though not all that he created remains, and modern development has swept away a few structures, the mark he left is indelible, and his name will forever be etched on the stones he transported from London and laid here with such zeal and enthusiasm in the latter half of the nineteenth century. Charles Harper, in his 1905 book *The Dorset Coast*, summarised his qualities by declaring him to be 'the amazing Burt, in whose nature eccentricity and business capacity, and the instincts of the pedagogue, the philanthropist and the money-maker seem to have been strangely mixed.'

George Burt was born in 1816, the son of Robert Burt, a stonemason, and Laetitia, the sister-in-law of John Mowlem, a quarryman's apprentice. Mowlem later paved London's streets with Purbeck stone, founding his fortune and the building contractor's firm which still bears his name. In a sense, George Burt merely followed in his uncle's footsteps, for it was John Mowlem who gave Swanage its first new architectural attractions, starting in 1862 with his Alfred Monument (OS REF: 195 SZ 033 787). This consists of a Tuscan column surmounted by four Russian cannon balls removed from the hulls of ships returning from the Crimean War. Mowlem let hero worship run away with him when composing its inscription:

'In commemoration of a great naval battle fought with the Danes in Swanage Bay by Alfred the Great, AD 877'.

It is probable that Alfred never actually engaged with the Danes, and that the Viking fleet was wrecked off Peveril Point in a storm. Fittingly, the monument now stands on the seafront next to the theatre named after this great admirer of the Saxon king.

Burt's reputation was built on being well-placed to add to his uncle's legacy. In the same year as Mowlem built the Alfred Monument, Burt erected an obelisk beside the road leading to Swanage in honour of Prince Albert, who had died the previous

The Ulwell Obelisk, Ballard Down, built by George Burt in 1892.

November. The obelisk's (OS REF: 195 SZ 033 787) subsequent history is less glorious, being shunted around in pieces to various sites and left to rot. Finally, in 1986 it was symbolically re-united with his lamenting widow in the form of a statue of Queen Victoria, minus a segment of stone, in front of a block of a flats which had been converted from the Royal Victoria Hotel.

A second obelisk in danger of sharing a similar fate was the Ulwell Obelisk (OS REF: 195 SZ 022 814) on Ballard Down, put up by George Burt in 1892 to commemorate the construction of a reservoir. He rescued it from near the Mansion House and the church of St Mary Woolnoth on the corner of King William and Lombard Streets in the City of London. It stood on the Purbecks for nearly fifty years before being taken down in about 1941, though the inscription on its base incorrectly says '1944'. It was re-erected in the course of two days in 1973 as part of a 'Military Aid for the Civil Community' project, though the impetus came from Bishop George Snow and his brother Brigadier John Snow. A plaque commemorates the event, the final stage of which involved the accompaniment of a Scots piper:

THE OBELISK
WAS DEMOLISHED IN 1944 TO AVOID
ITS BEING OF ASSISTANCE TO ENEMY
AIRCRAFT IN DURING THE WAR.
IT WAS RE-ERECTED BY MEN OF 129
(E.RIDING) FIELD SQUADRON ROYAL
ENGINEERS (VOLUNTEERS) UNDER THE
DIRECTION OF CAPT. R. ALTON RE
THE LOWEST SECTION WAS FOUND CRACKED
AND WAS MOUNTED BESIDE THE OBELISK
11.VII.73

This disconnected section took about four feet off the original height of thirty feet. Originally there was a long inscription which commemorated Burt's endeavours in removing it from outside the Mansion House and his bringing water to Swanage, but the inscription now reveals nothing of its origins, only its height above sea level (489 feet).

Burt's first major addition to Swanage's architecture was the Wellington Clock Tower (OS REF: 195 SZ 037 787) which originally stood at the southern approach to London Bridge. Designed by Arthur Ashpitel, it was erected in 1854 by public subscription soon after the death of the Duke of Wellington at a cost of £700. A canopy was built at the top to shelter a statue of the Duke, but the statue was never installed. The tower clock kept bad time when it was in London, possibly due to the rumble of the traffic. Ironically, it was the increase in traffic that sealed the tower's fate, as it had become an obstruction.

The clock never made it to Swanage, but Burt removed the tower free of charge in 1867, bringing it in pieces by sea and then presenting it to his friend Thomas Docwra to erect in the grounds of his house, The Grove. Docwra paid £1,000 to put it back up, considerably more than its original cost. When it became unsafe in 1904, the spire was replaced by a cupola. The Grove's garden was turned into a public garden, in which the Grosvenor Hotel was later built - though that too has since been demolished.

As long as it has been in Swanage, the Wellington Clock Tower has remained in the same position on the south shore near Peveril Point, but it has seen many changes around it. The latest development came

Purbeck House, Swanage, rebuilt by George Burt in the 1880s,
and which incorporates fragments from Billingsgate Fish Market.

in the 1980s when a community of red-roofed and white-walled
Spanish style villas was strikingly juxtaposed against it.

The Grosvenor Hotel also boasted two fluted Ionic Columns,
slightly truncated, as well as another fragment in the same style. They
are reputed to have come from a building in Regent Street, London,
possibly designed by Charles Cockerell, who designed the Ashmolean
Museum in Oxford, and whose style they are typical of. Following the
demolition of the Grosvenor Hotel, the columns were kept in store
until 1996 when the Prince Albert Gardens were redeveloped by
Purbeck District Council to form part of the Swanage Seafront
Improvement Scheme. The two complete columns, with the fragment
to one side, form the focal point of an amphitheatre in the form of
circular patio of polished paving stones and several rows of seating
around the edge.

Burt started shipping London down to Dorset in earnest when he
began winning major contracts to rebuild the capital. One such
contract was the rebuilding of Billingsgate Fish Market in 1874, and
the resulting demolition of the existing building meant that Swanage
gained a number of items. Burt's work at Billingsgate coincided with
his decision to rebuild Purbeck House (OS REF: 195 SZ 028 787), in
which he had lived for seventeen years, to a design by George

Rackstrow Crickmay. What resulted was a fairly unattractive building in what might be called the 'baronial' style.

In one corner there is a tower which contains the initials 'GB' and his motto 'Know Thyself' inscribed in the stone. In the other corner, down the hill, is an octagonal gazebo topped with a cupola and Burt's coat-of-arms. Its original weather-vane, a gilded flying fish from Billingsgate, was removed when it became unsafe. The gazebo is entered from below by a spiral staircase and has a door knocker taken from Montague House, Bloomsbury.

Some of the oddments salvaged by Burt from various London contracts have disappeared, including a scale model of Cleopatra's needle and a jawbone of a whale, but many remain: In the stable yard, an iron column from Billingsgate supports the porch; inserted high up on the façade there is the so-called Parthenon Frieze, probably coming from a London exhibition. From the same batch of iron columns a balustrade was built with a total of six iron columns, eight and a half feet high. Five border what was the tennis court at the top of the garden, one of which is surmounted by a pair of tennis racket frames, and three others have cannon-balls on top.

Perhaps the only item that was both built by Burt in its original site as well as moved later to Swanage is the rusticated and vermiculated stone arch from Grosvenor Place near Hyde Park Corner. Four feet wide and eight feet high, its inscription records its removal in 1883 along with a statue of the Duke of Wellington which stood close to his residence, Apsley House - though the statue was probably never brought to Swanage. The keystone of the arch is said to be Burt's own carving of the face of a river god, or possibly Neptune, but the carving lost part of its beard when struck by lightning.

The Royal Exchange building site in the City also resulted in several statues making their way to Purbeck House, and which now stand next to the former tennis court. One is robed, probably a cleric, whilst the other two without heads are supposed to represent Charles I and II in Roman garb, though they may in fact be closer to likenesses of Henry V and Edward I.

Up a double flight of steps lies the so-called 'temple', which is more of a summer-house. It has a pagoda-like roof, curving gently upwards and crowned by two terracotta-winged dragons facing away from

The Town Hall, Swanage, showing the seventeenth century facade originally attached to the Mercer's Hall in Cheapside.

each other. The building incorporates eight Doric columns from the toll-house removed in 1878 from Waterloo Bridge, and the floor is paved with tiles from the lobby of the Houses of Parliament, removed when Mowlems carried out some work there in 1880.

The odd one out of all the features in the garden of Purbeck House is the rotunda, which lays no claim to have been reincarnated in Swanage, though where its stones came from we do not know. It contains the wheel from a wagon for transporting Purbeck stone, a trade in which Mowlems ironically played no part, but saw decline from close quarters. In 1935 Purbeck House was taken over by the sisters of the Convent of Our Lady of Mercy, and it has recently been converted into a hotel which allows free access to the grounds.

A little way down the High Street from Purbeck House is a seventeenth century façade which used to be attached to the Mercer's Hall in Cheapside in the City and now presents a magnificent front to Swanage Town Hall. When it was necessary to rebuild the hall as part of the widening of Cheapside, the façade was considered too dirty, and was replaced by a replica. The original in Swanage bears the emblem of the Mercer's Company over the door - two cherubs covering the Virgin's head. On the first floor, a door opens onto a balcony, and the date 1670 is visible on the base of each stanchion. The broken pediment has survived, but not, alas, the statues of Faith, Hope and Charity. A clock which was not part of the original design has been attached, whilst inside the Council Chamber there are busts of John Mowlem and George Burt.

Despite all his architectural reclamation, Burt had yet to stamp his own idiosyncratic style on the town by designing a new building. To do this, Burt bought a tract of 80 acres stretching from Swanage to Durlston Head. Ambitious plans were hatched with the architect Crickmay for what was to be called Durlston Park Estate, with roads, shops and private villas. Thankfully Durlston Castle was not to be crowded out by development, for little was built apart from a few seats, a couple of which are inscribed in memory of the Encombe aristocrats Lord Eldon and Baron Stowell.

As for Durlston Castle (OS REF: 195 SZ 034 773), it is more of a seaside pavilion of the style that might have graced a pier at nearby Bournemouth. It has some fine turrets, a panelled interior and bollards from Trafalgar Square at the entrance, but it was savaged by Charles Harper in *The Dorset Coast* as 'a hideous place that could have been built by a humorist'. Harper misunderstood Burt's motives, his wish to enlighten and educate his fellow men, or his character, which did not include a noticeable sense of humour.

High up on the lower wall is a sundial beneath which are two large stone plaques, inscribed 'DURATION OF LONGEST DAY & CLOCK TIMES OF THE WORLD' and 'CONVEXITY OF THE OCEAN & TIDES', each of which record numerous chronological, geophysical and scientific data. Burt's pedagogical pretensions are shown again in a third plaque, further down the hill and fixed to another rampart, and which has distances to far-away places in rings from Durlston Head.

The real *pièce de resistance* of Durlston's open-air classroom is the Great Globe (OS REF: 195 SZ 034 773) (see the illustration on page 79). Ten feet in diameter, weighing forty tons, it consists of fifteen segments of Portland Stone which were hewn in Mowlem's stoneyard in Greenwich and are held in position by granite dowels. It still shows the oceans and continents, with British colonial possessions prominent, understandable in an era when Britain was at the height of its power. Despite being sculpted in 1887 and standing in a site exposed to the elements, the features are still clear.

The Globe stands in a kind of large open niche, on the back wall of which there are inscribed tablets with astronomical information and the writings of several poets, including Shakespeare, Milton, and Wordsworth. Burt could not have chosen a better place to evoke a point of departure for the lands and oceans he so rigorously depicted in his maps and catalogued on his tablets, for on a fine day the view is of sea and sky and boats moving to and fro in the Channel.

A little to the west of Durlston Head are the Tilly Whim Caves, where John Mowlem worked the stone as a boy. On the cliff face above these disused quarry entrances Burt engraved the lines from Shakespeare's *Tempest*, singularly appropriate to Burt himself, this wind-swept spot and the whole subject of follies:

The cloud-capp'd towers, the gorgeous palaces,
The solemn temples, the great globe itself,
Yea all which it inherit, shall dissolve,
And, like this insubstantial pageant faded,
Leave not a rack behind.

The same lines were engraved on a smaller granite globe, just three feet in diameter, which Burt had made in 1879, and which now can be found in the garden of the house bought by his grandson on the banks of the Beaulieu River in Hampshire.

What was Burt like as a person? Apart from his stones and their inscriptions, his character remains strangely elusive. A little can be gleaned from Thomas Hardy, who attended a meeting of the Dorset Field Club at Durlston Castle in 1892, where he met 'Old Mr B, the King of Swanage [who] had a good profile but was rougher in his speech that I should have expected after his years in London - being the ordinary type of Dorset man, self-made by trade'. That same day Burt declared in a speech that he believed in a future for Swanage, and that may well have been the prime motive for his many improvements. Pleasure through education was his watchword, and the desire to leave a legacy of learning which was so much a hallmark of many Victorians. The contribution of Burt to Swanage has not been equalled since, nor has any other Dorset town benefited from such philanthropy by a single man.

The gazebo at Borough House in this pleasant market town was originally built to overlook open countryside, land which has since become the wide-lawned Redcotts Recreation Ground. Borough House is an eighteenth century house which was originally owned by the Ellis family, brewers who built the gazebo in about 1750. In the twentieth century Borough House was cannibalised into the Tivoli Cinema and a few shops. Closed for a long period in the 1970s and 80s, the site became badly neglected and the gazebo was left to the vandals, though the Tivoli subsequently reopened.

In 1984-5 the gazebo was renovated by the Wimborne Civic Society whose founding date, 1973, was engraved into one of its panes of glass. It is a two-storey building constructed with red bricks and a clay tile roof. The grand entrance is by means of a curving staircase to the upper floor, the interior of which is exquisitely gothicised, including a carpet with a gothic window pattern, and some fine panelling. The finest feature is the bay window which was originally flush with the wall that the gazebo forms part of, but was remodelled, along with other major reconstruction work by retired Canford School art master Robin Noscoe, and the gazebo now contains the Wimborne Civic Society's archives and hosts small meetings and exhibitions.

The gazebo, Borough House, Wimborne Minster.

Situated some eight miles north of Wimborne, the St Giles estate has been in the Ashley-Cooper family since the Norman Conquest. The present St Giles House replaced an earlier house and was begun in 1650 by the 1st Earl of Shaftesbury, whose political prominence led to him becoming one of the founders of the Whig party.

Also prominent among his descendants was his grandson, the 3rd Earl, Anthony Ashley-Cooper (1671-1713), a philosopher who published *Letters Concerning Enthusiasm* and *The Moralists*. The latter appeared in 1709, and clearly reflected the psychology that underlay eighteenth century aesthetics. Shaftesbury also foreshadowed much of the thinking behind the building of follies as the expression of art in nature, conceiving 'Ideal Nature' as a state of perfect beauty theoretically existing in the distant past before the 'Creation of Man', a state which the artist has the duty to recreate.

Much of Shaftesbury's philosophising is thought to have been done in what is now known as the Philosopher's Tower (OS REF: 195 SU 046 111), built in about 1700. Isolated in a field far from the house, but close to the road between Wimborne and Cranborne, the tower is built of red brick and its south side carries a carved stone cartouche of the arms of the 3rd Earl, showing Ashley-Cooper marrying Manners.

In about 1750 the 4th Earl implemented his father's ideas by

The Philosopher's Tower, built by the 3rd Earl of Shaftesbury in about 1700.

The Castellated Archway, St Giles House.

building a rococo style garden to complement St Giles House, including a number of follies which contrasted with the formal beech avenues and hedges, and a sunken garden. The serpentine naturalness embraced a sham castle, cascade, thatched house, round pavilion on a mount and Chinese bridge complete with a small pagoda on its apex, but all of these have long gone. Of the surviving features, the Castellated Archway (OS REF: 195 SU 030 115) is a piece of pure decoration, apparently leading nowhere and so much more a folly for that. Presumed to date from 1748, it consists of two circular embattled towers connected by an arch, made mainly of ashlar with dark bands of heathstone rustication.

One visitor was the diarist Bishop Pococke who noted in 1754 a piece of literary furniture in a landscape which strived to be different from the styles that had gone before: 'a round pavilion on a Mount, Shake Spears house, in which is a small statue of him & his works in a Glass case; & in all the houses & seats are books in hanging Glass cases.'

Pococke also recorded what was perhaps the 4th Earl's greatest work: 'there is a most beautiful grotto finished by Mr Castles of Marybone - it consists of a winding walk and ante room. These are mostly made of Rock sparke, adorn'd with Moss. In the inner room is a great variety of most beautiful shells, petrifications and fine polished pebble.'

Indeed the Grotto (OS REF: 195 SU 035 114) was a fine sight, even boasting oyster shells with real pearls, fossils, coral and stone flakes mounted on a timber framework, but it is not like that today. Standing just above the top end of a narrow part of the lake, but without any running water, the exterior has a ragged façade reminiscent of the style of the leading eighteenth century grotto and arbour designer, Thomas Wright. The roof, however, is not typically Wright, being mainly slate, with a few red tiles and a chimney pot of the same colour. The Grotto consists of four chambers, including an anteroom and two side wings of no significance, while the main chamber consists of a brick shell faced internally with tufa. It is still remarkable for its wildly undulating walls and ceilings, which follow the natural form of the branches used in the construction, and on which remain a few shells and coral fans, giving the impression of the surface of an underwater reef. There are ledges for candles, as well as a fireplace added in the late nineteenth century.

The Grotto is linked with Susan, the daughter of the Earl of Gainsborough, who married the 4th Earl at the age of fourteen, and whose portrait used to hang in the house, showing a slender, fair-haired girl with a pensive face. She and her husband were great patrons of the arts, and are reputed to have entertained George Frederick Handel for tea in the Grotto. All in all, the Shaftesburys spent the then enormous sum of £10,000, some of which went to an unknown Italian artist so shy or nervous he would not let anyone see him work. Although the Grotto was restored in 1959 by a Miss Jebb and a Miss Sant, it has tragically degraded to the point that it now urgently needs to be saved from the likelihood of collapse.

The Grotto, St Giles House.

FURTHER READING

Barton, Stuart, *Monumental Follies* (Lyle Publications), 1972

Darke, Jo, *The Monument Guide to England & Wales* (Macdonald Illustrated), 1991

Eyres, Patrick (Ed.), *Four Purbeck Arcadias* (New Arcadia Press), 45/46 1998

Jones, Barbara, *Follies and Grottoes* (Constable) 1974

Hansell, Peter & Jean, *Doves and Dovecotes* (Millstream Books)

Headley, Gwyn & Meulenkamp, Wim, *Follies*, 2nd Edition (Aurum Press), 1999

Kay-Robinson, Denys, *The Landscape of Thomas Hardy* (Webb & Bower), 1984

Lewer, David & Calkin, J. Bernard, *Curiosities of Swanage or Old London By The Sea* (The Gavin Press), 1986

Osborn, George, *Dorset Curiosities* (Dovecote Press), 1986

Pevsner, Nikolaus, *The Buildings of England*, series (Penguin)

Royal Commission on Historic Monuments, Dorset, London, 1908 & 1952-72

Treves, Frederick, *Highways and Byways of Dorset*,1906

Whitelaw, Jeffery W., *Follies* (Shire Publications) 1982

The following publications have also been a help: Victoria County History; *Country Life*; *Follies*, organ of the Folly Fellowship; *Garden History*, journal of the Garden History Society.

THE FOLLY FELLOWSHIP is a registered charity dedicated to the protection and preservation for the benefit of the public the historical, architectural and constructional heritage existing in and around follies, grottoes and garden buildings. Any reader wishing to know more about the Fellowship, should address their enquiry to: The Secretary, 7 Inch's Yard, Market Street, Newbury, Berkshire RG14 5DP.

ACKNOWLEDGEMENTS

In researching this book the vast majority of the owners of the follies have been very helpful and obliging. That generosity of spirit may not extend to anyone who attempts to trespass. Most of Dorset's follies are either easily visible from public roads, or can be approached on public footpaths. Landowners are usually willing to allow access to those who are genuinely interested in follies, but it is important to ask permission before venturing onto private land.

The following people have been particularly helpful in the research for this book, but they do not represent a comprehensive list, and no offence is meant if anyone has not been mentioned: Jeremy Barker, Sylvia Beamon, Pieter and Rita Boogaart, Mike Cousins, Graham Davies, Gwyn Headley, Robin Noscoe, Wim Meulenkamp.

I have taken many of the photographs myself, and others come from the Dovecote Press Collection, but a special debt is owed to the following for allowing the inclusion of illustrations in their possession or for which they hold the copyright. The British Library: page 65; Dorset County Museum: page 25; Royal Commission Historical Monuments (England) © Crown Copyright: pages 23, 33, 46, 53, 76, 77.

The Great Globe, Swanage.

The

DISCOVER DORSET

Series of Books

A series of paperback books providing informative illustrated
introductions to Dorset's history, culture and way of life.
The following titles have so far been published.

BRIDGES *David McFetrich and Jo Parsons*

CASTLES AND FORTS *Colin Pomeroy*

CRANBORNE CHASE *Desmond Hawkins*

FARMING *J.H.Bettey*

FOLLIES *Jonathan Holt*

FOSSILS *Richard Edmonds*

GEOLOGY *Paul Ensom*

THE GEORGIANS *Jo Draper*

THE INDUSTRIAL PAST *Peter Stanier*

ISLE OF PURBECK *Paul Hyland*

LEGENDS *Jeremy Harte*

MILLS *Peter Stanier*

PORTLAND *Stuart Morris*

POTTERY *Penny Copland-Griffiths*

THE PREHISTORIC AGE *Bill Putnam*

REGENCY, RIOT AND REFORM *Jo Draper*

THE ROMANS *Bill Putnam*

SAXONS AND VIKINGS *David Hinton*

SHIPWRECKS *Maureen Attwooll*

STONE QUARRYING *Jo Thomas*

THE VICTORIANS *Jude James*

All the books about Dorset published by The Dovecote Press
are available in bookshops throughout the county,
or in case of difficulty direct from the publishers.
The Dovecote Press Ltd, Stanbridge,
Wimborne, Dorset BH21 4JD
Tel: 01258 840549 www.dovecotepress.com